SNOWBOARDING

SNOWBOARDING

THE ULTIMATE FREERIDE

MIKE FABBRO

illustrations by Oliver Roy

M&S

This book is dedicated
to all those who have,
in some way, shared
their snowboarding
thoughts, adventures,
and experiences
with me. Without your
enthusiasm and love
for the sport, this
book would not
have been possible.

This book is also
dedicated to Norma,
because the only
thing better than great
riding, is great riding
with a friend. Norma
is my best friend.

Canadian Cataloguing in Publication Data

Fabbro, Mike.
    Snowboarding : the ultimate freeride

Includes index.
ISBN 0-7710-3122-X

1. Snowboarding.   I. Title

GV857 .S57F32 1996   796.9   C96-931744-1

Typesetting by M&S, Toronto

The publishers acknowledge the support of the Canada Council and the Ontario Arts Council for their publishing program.

Printed and bound in Canada

McClelland & Stewart Inc.
The Canadian Publishers
481 University Avenue
Toronto, Ontario
M5G 2E9

1 2 3 4 5   00 99 98 97 96

CONTENTS

INTRODUCTION

PASSION COMES IN MANY FORMS

Snowboarding is the best excuse for enjoying snow since the snowball fight. It blends the fun and challenge of surfing, skateboarding, and skiing. It's the hottest addiction on the planet — and it's 100 per cent legal. In a world that is becoming increasingly complex, the simplicity, purity, and steep learning curve of snowboarding is winning the hearts and imaginations of riders, young and old alike. Almost anyone can learn in just a few hours, and every session delivers spills and thrills.

In less than ten years, snowboarding has evolved from a fringe activity to a mainstream sport. Its growth is unparalleled, and with its introduction as a full-medal event at the 1998 Olympic Games, in Nagano, Japan, the best is yet to come. Interest in snowboarding is growing, the demand for snowboarding products is growing, and so is the demand for information on the sport.

> "THE ULTIMATE FREERIDE IS ABOUT SNOW-BOARDING; ALL KINDS OF SNOWBOARDING IN ALL KINDS OF PLACES. IT ISN'T ABOUT RACING — SOMEONE ELSE CAN WRITE THAT BOOK."

Soon after I started snowboarding, in 1988, I started writing about it. I couldn't say enough great things about my new discovery, and I wanted to share my experiences. That's when I started getting questions on how to get started, what equipment was best, how to ride different types of terrain, and questions about competitions, culture, and everything in between. I thought that with the passage of time, these and other questions would be answered by magazines, the industry, and by the riders themselves. It's happening, but it isn't keeping pace with the growth of the sport — there's still an information vacuum.

That's why I decided to write a book. Once I got started, I found the hardest part was deciding what to include and what to leave out. So I went to the source — the riders — and asked what they wanted. They told me they didn't want it to be a very detailed "how to" book with glossy photos, and I agreed. The "how to" of the sport is being constantly developed by riders, who continually push themselves and their equipment. As equipment improves, so do they, and so do their techniques. The riding techniques I describe in this book are the unchanging fundamental principles of snowboarding.

The content of this book reflects the input of average riders, but isn't limited to it. It also reflects years of on-hill testing and feedback from some of the world's hottest pros. It's full of practical information, with chapters that can be read in any sequence or from beginning to end. It doesn't preach on how to dress, act, or ride, it encourages you to ride the way you want, just better. Regardless of your age, sex, size, or snowboarding experience, this book has something for you.

I have tried to simplify the information and present it in a way that will be quick to read and easy to understand — I am fully aware that snowboarders would much rather ride than read about it!

This book is no substitute for an early-season session in fresh powder, but it can go wherever you go: a quick reference and your loyal companion. It will help you make the most of your riding experience and will never snake your line.

JUST A FEW REASONS TO SNOWBOARD:

1. IT'S FUN!
2. IT'S GREAT EXERCISE.
3. YOU CAN DO IT BACKWARDS.
4. NO MATTER HOW OLD YOU ARE, YOU FEEL LIKE A KID.
5. BECAUSE YOU CAN!

AND FOR SKIERS, ADD:

6. NO COLD HANDS OR FEET, EVER AGAIN.
7. NO SORE FEET, EVER AGAIN.

CHAPTER 1

OUR ROOTS

The sport of snowboarding is still so young its history is unfolding as you read this book. Although there may be differing accounts of how and why the sport evolved the way it has, most agree it has its roots in surfing. The exhilaration and free spiritedness of challenging nature's elements were a seductive lure to surfers. There was just one problem: good surfing wasn't widely accessible on demand. This void inspired the development of other activities that eventually became sports. First, they surfed the concrete, and skateboarding was born. Then they surfed the wind when the waves weren't abundant, and windsurfing came to be. Eventually, all of these activities inspired the extremists to surf powder snow in their quest to capture the sideways-standing feeling of surfing that is difficult to describe in words. Once on the snow, the influence of skiing and skiers, in terms of technology and technique, was inevitable – and "skiboarding" was born.

HALL OF FAME

HERE IS A LIST OF SOME OF THE STARS I WOULD ELECT TO A SNOWBOARDING HALL OF FAME. THE LIST IS SHORT BECAUSE THE SPORT IS SO YOUNG. ALL THE RIDERS ARE STILL VERY DEDICATED SNOWBOARDERS AND CONTINUE TO INFLUENCE THE SPORT.

TOM SIMS & JAKE CARPENTER

FOR THEIR PIONEERING WORK IN DEVELOPING THE MODERN SNOWBOARD.
(SEE PAGES 7 TO 9)

TERRY KIDWELL

REFERRED TO AS THE FATHER OF FREESTYLE BY SNOWBOARDER MAGAZINE, TERRY IS CREDITED WITH HAVING THE WORLD'S FIRST SIGNATURE MODEL. HIS FIRST EXPERIENCE OF SNOWBOARDING WAS ON A WATER-SKI IN

1978-79. IN 1980, HE RODE A WINTERSTICK AND TOOK OFF THE METAL FIN SO HE COULD DO BASIC FREESTYLE TRICKS.

IN 1982 HE MET TOM SIMS RIDING A RAVINE AT TAHOE, NEVADA, AND EVENTUALLY BECAME A TEAM RIDER. TERRY CONVINCED THE DESIGNERS AT SIMS TO ROUND OFF THE TAIL ON HIS BOARD FOR BETTER FREESTYLE PERFORMANCE. HE WENT ON TO WIN HIS FIRST WORLD CHAMPIONSHIP IN THE HALFPIPE AT THE 1984 SODA SPRINGS CHAMPIONSHIPS. WHEN HE RETIRED FROM COMPETITION IN THE LATE EIGHTIES, HE HAD WON FOUR WORLD CHAMPIONSHIPS AND THREE OVERALL WORLD TITLES IN FREESTYLE. TERRY HAD A SOLID SKI BACKGROUND, WHICH ALSO HELPED HIM WIN THE OCCASIONAL ALPINE TITLE. HE STILL RIDES WITH THE BEST OF THEM.

There are several events and individuals that deserve a page in the history book of snowboarding. I have tried to give you a brief overview of the evolution of snowboarding. I recognize that what follows may be too brief for some, so I apologize in advance to all those I've omitted who have left their mark on the world stage of snowboarding. Your good karma is still with us.

IT ALL STARTED WITH . . .

THE SNURFER: Sherman Poppens, of Michigan, invented the Snurfer by screwing two skis together for his kids. Poppens worked for Brunswick, a company that amongst other things made bowling alleys, and he eventually used equipment at Brunswick to refine his Snurfers. The boards were very simple: they were plywood, had non-skid pads for the feet (no foot straps or bindings), and had a rope with a handle attached to the nose (no edges or P-Tex).

Poppens sold the rights of his Snurfer to Brunswick in 1966, when the popularity of surfing was soaring and skateboarding was being discovered. Brunswick mass-produced and marketed the Snurfer and sold over 100,000 units. The Snurfer sold for $19.95 and was marketed as a toy.

Nevertheless, the world's first Snurfer contest was held in Muskegon, Michigan, on February 18, 1968. The race had a running start and was a straight downhill. This contest continued until 1979 and set the competitive stage of snowboarding for today. This last Snurfer contest was won by one Jake Burton Carpenter on a modified Snurfer.

WINTERSTICK: In 1969 Dimitrije Milovich, a core surfer living in Utah, produced a molded polyester snowboard that looked like a surfboard for snow and called it the Winterstick. In 1975, he founded his own company and started producing boards with a large spoon-shaped nose with both round and swallow tails. These models were said to be the best powder boards of their day.

Although Milovich brought snowboarding to a new level of public awareness, he suffered financially and stopped producing boards in 1984.

BURTON: In 1968, when Jake Burton Carpenter was fourteen, he got a Snurfer for Christmas. Jake experimented with his Snurfer, but continued to dedicate himself to kneeboarding and skiing until he had graduated from college. Motivated by his experience with the Snurfer, his background in skiing, and his frustration with corporate life (he worked as an assistant at a Manhattan investment firm), Jake started a snowboard company in Londonderry, Vermont. The year was

1977, and the boards bore the name Burton.

Jake was an entrepreneur and an innovator. He continually refined his shapes and his construction and manu-facturing techniques. His early models included wood laminates with adjustable front bindings, surfboard-shaped fiber-glass models, and wide, swallow-tail shapes with long fins for powder.

Jake's contributions to snowboard-ing went beyond design and production. He knew that for his boards to sell, he had to convince the ski industry that snowboarding was a sport — that his boards were not toys. He was relentless with his "sport first" attitude to pro-moting his products, and it payed off.

Jake worked with ski centers to educate them on all aspects of snowboarding and organized competitions. With acceptance came the market, and with the market came competition.

SIMS: According to Tom Sims, he made his first snowboard as a woodworking project in 1963. It was made of laminat-ed wood, had carpet nailed to the deck, had a wood runner and a sheet of alu-minum on the base. He called it a skate-board for the snow. In 1966 Tom started surfing, which influenced his later snowboard projects.

In the Seventies' skateboarding boom, Tom won a world championship and started producing his own "decks."

He kept experimenting with snowboard designs, but it wasn't until 1978, when he collaborated with Chuck Barfoot, a Sims research-and-development man with a surfing background, that he produced his first real prototype. It was a powder machine – a swallow-tail board similar to Milovich's Winterstick.

Tom sold Sims Snowboards to Umbro Sports International, where he is currently employed as a technical consultant.

CONTESTS

The first (unofficial) world snowboard championship took place in Soda Springs, California, in March 1983. Tom Sims, who had just added steel edges to his board, won the slalom event, placed second in the downhill, and third in the halfpipe/ravine contest.

World championships have been held every year since, which helped the sport gain Olympic status for the 1998 winter games.

EUROPE

The snowboarding scene in Europe was taking a different but parallel path. In the mid-Eighties, José Fernandes, a one-time Swiss skateboarding champion, was instrumental in developing European interest in snowboarding. He used a modified ski-touring binding and

WORLD CUP CHAMPIONSHIPS IN 1992 AT THE AGE OF 18. HE WON IT AGAIN IN '94. HE ALSO WON THE '93 AND '95 WORLD CHAMPIONSHIPS, ALL IN THE HALFPIPE. HIS PRESENCE ON THE WORLD SCENE MARKS THE END OF AMERICAN DOMINATION OF THE FREESTYLE EVENTS AND THE BEGINNING OF SINGLE-EVENT SPECIALISTS. HIS RIDING STYLE WAS FAST AND STRONG. HE WAS A TECHNICALLY ADVANCED FREERIDER WHO WOULD NOT ONLY DO TRICKS BIGGER THAN MOST, BUT DO THEM SWITCH. HIS PERFORMANCES INSPIRED A SERIES OF RED-HOT FREESTYLE RIDERS FROM SCANDINAVIA AND EUROPE.

MARTIN FREINADEMETZ

BORN IN AUSTRIA IN 1970, MARTIN IS CONSIDERED A VETERAN ON THE ISF PRO-RACING TOUR. DURING HIS

EARLY SNOWBOARDING YEARS, HE ONLY FREERODE AND LOVED TO RIDE POWDER. HE ENTERED HIS FIRST RACE SO HE COULD "PARTY AND MEET GIRLS," AND SURPRISED HIMSELF WHEN HE PLACED FOURTH. HIS SECOND RACE WAS THE AUSTRIAN CHAMPIONSHIPS IN 1988, WHERE HE PLACED SECOND.

FROM THEN ON, HE WAS HOOKED ON RACING AND BEGAN DOMINATING WORLD CUP ALPINE RACING. IN THE 1995 WORLD CHAMPIONSHIPS, IN DAVOS, SWITZERLAND, HE WON BOTH THE SUPER G AND THE SLALOM EVENTS – A DISTINCTION ONLY HE CAN CLAIM. LATER THE SAME YEAR, HE WON THE EXTREME DOWNHILL CHAMPI-ONSHIPS IN VALDEZ, ALASKA. MARTIN CONTINUES TO LOVE RACING, HAS FUN DOING IT, AND ADDS A UNIQUE BLEND OF COLOR AND PERSONALITY TO ALPINE EVENTS.

ski boots on his snowboard and started winning contests.

This was the start of the Euro-carving scene, a period where the Europeans rode with extreme binding angles, narrow race boards, and a ski technique to carve deep turns at high speeds. It was a time when the Europeans dominated the alpine racing events and the Americans reigned supreme in freestyle events. That has since changed.

CHAPTER 2

THE WHOLE SNOWBOARD: THE SUM OF ITS PARTS

Knowing the technical terms in this chapter won't make you a better rider, but it will help you understand how and why your equipment was designed the way it was.

RUNNING LENGTH (also referred to as board length): Normally the length of the board from tip to tail (measured in centimeters).

EFFECTIVE EDGE: The distance between the widest point of the nose to the widest point of the tail of your board (measured in centimeters).

CONTACT LENGTH: The distance between the points where the front and back of your board make contact with the snow (measured in centimeters). This measurement is similar to effective edge, but it is a better indicator for comparing boards' performance

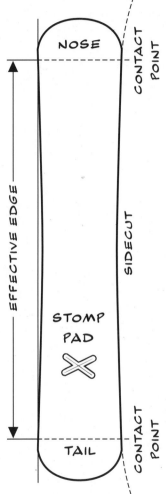

characteristics. The longer contact length, the more stable the board will be. Short contact lengths are great for spinning and freestyle.

CAMBER: The arch in your board. It provides your board with its spring and gives it a snappy feel. The camber helps you when turning, spinning, and jumping.

STANCE WIDTH: The distance between the center points of both your bindings (usually measured in inches).

STANCE ANGLES: The angle your binding makes with an imaginary line drawn across your board. A zero-zero stance is straight across the board. The first angle always refers to the front foot.

WAIST: The narrowest part of the board (measured in centimeters).

SIDECUT: The shape cut into the sides of your board. It is measured as the radius of a circle that would fit into the side profile of your board. Sidecuts can be both symmetric, with the waist in the center (twin tip and freeride boards), and parabolic, with the waist back of center (some freeride, freecarve, and race boards). The smaller the measurement, the deeper the sidecut, producing a more responsive board. Sidecut and flex pattern are always designed together, so examine both together.

FLEX: The pressure required to bend a board out of its resting position. Boards with a stiff flex require more pressure to bend them and are good for heavy riders or for riders looking for performance at high speeds. A board with a soft flex, like a freestyle board, is forgiving and easy to ride.

FLEX PATTERN: The shape your board makes when it is flexed. Some patterns are constant from tip to tail and some are elliptical (softer in the tip, and stiffer in the tail area). Twin-tip boards should have constant flex patterns and directional boards should have slightly elliptical flex patterns.

STOMP PAD: A stomp pad is a non-skid pad used to improve traction between your back boot and your board when your back foot is out of its binding. These pads are inexpensive, come in a variety of shapes and colors, and are self-adhesive.

LEASH: Leashes are for dogs, except in snowboarding, where some ski centers still require "retention devices" for insurance purposes. Because snow-board bindings don't release (making "retention devices" redundant), leashes serve little purpose, except to make a good shoulder strap.

Chapter 3

BOOTS, BOARDS, AND BINDINGS

BOOTS: LESS SHOE, MORE SOUL

Boots have come a long way since the early days of the snowmobile specials wrapped with duct tape. Today's snowboarding boots are designed with the specific demands of the sport in mind.

Most of them are comfortable and warm, but performance, adjustability, and durability will vary.

The challenge for boot designers has been to avoid bulky footwear without compromising function, comfort, and warmth — and many have done it.

FREESTYLE BOOTS are the shortest, softest, and lightest models, designed to be flexible for doing freestyle tricks. Some have no liner and look more like basketball shoes than snowboarding boots. Their advantages are light weight and flexibility; their disadvantages are that they may be too soft for all-terrain performance, and they take longer to dry because they don't have removable liners.

A HOT TIP

YOU CAN KEEP THE LEATHER PARTS OF YOUR BOOTS, GLOVES, OR MITTS DRY BY PROTECTING THEM WITH A SEALING PRODUCT. WAXY PRODUCTS LIKE MINK OIL OR DUBBIN LAST LONGER THAN LIQUID SILICONE LEATHER PROTECTORS. APPLY A GENEROUS AMOUNT OF THE WAX PROTECTOR AND RUB IT IN. TO IMPROVE PENETRATION, YOU CAN HEAT THE WAX GENTLY WITH A HAIRDRYER. ONCE IT'S DRY, APPLY A SECOND COAT. A TIN OF A GOOD LEATHER PROTECTOR COSTS AS LITTLE AS $3 AND SHOULD LAST ALL SEASON.

FREERIDING BOOTS are slightly heavier, thicker, and stiffer than freestyle boots, but not nearly as stiff as hard boots. They offer the support required for all-terrain riding, carving, and lofty jumps. Many models come with lace-up liners and adjustable Velcro straps to prevent heel lift.

HARD BOOTS are the stiffest (and heaviest) boots available. They come in race and freeride models, with the race models being the stiffest. They can only be used with plate bindings and are the choice of many freeriders, especially those with a skiing background.

WOMEN'S AND KID'S MODELS are now made by most manufacturers. The women's models have a shorter cuff, a narrower heel, and a higher arch than men's models.

BUYING TIPS: Buy your soft boots to fit with thin socks. When you have broken your liners in, you can switch to thicker socks. If you're prone to cold feet, stick with boots with liners — they are slightly thicker and offer more insulation.

CUSTOMIZING YOUR FIT: If you have a hard-to-fit foot, you can always buy custom-fitted insoles or liners.

BOARDS

FREESTYLE BOARDS come in directional and twin-tip shapes (see Chapter 4) and account for more than half the boards on the snow. They're short, wide, and are designed to be ridden on soft snow, in a halfpipe, and for jumping. They are easy to turn, spin very well, and have a very light feel. On the downside, they tend to perform poorly at high speeds and on ice.

FREERIDING BOARDS are almost always directional boards and are designed as all-terrain vehicles. Most are designed to be ridden with soft boots, but they can also be ridden with hard boots. Because these boards offer a wide range of performance, they are the popular choice of both today's progressive riders and snowboarding schools.

EXTREME OR ALL-MOUNTAIN BOARDS are longer versions of freeriding boards. They are designed for adrenaline junkies who blaze through powder, crank high-speed turns, and loft big airs off snowy ledges. They're long and strong — but with a soft flex.

TYPICAL BOARD LENGTHS

FREESTYLE: 145 TO 155 CM

FREERIDING: 155 TO 165 CM

EXTREME: 165 TO 180 CM

FREECARVING: 155 TO 167 CM

RACING: 155 TO 170 CM

These boards are the choice of heavier riders or backcountry riders who ride with a pack.

FREECARVING BOARDS are stiffer versions of freeriding boards that are designed to be ridden with hard boots. They have a deeper sidecut than freeriding boards, making them more responsive, and have a stiffer flex pattern. These boards perform well at speed and on hard or icy conditions, but are limited for freestyle.

RACE BOARDS are high-end performance machines designed to be ridden on a race course. The slalom models come in both symmetric and asymmetric shapes that range from 155 cm to 170 cm. Giant slalom (GS) and Super Giant Slalom (Super G) models range from 175 cm to 200 cm. Because these boards are extremely stiff and have very little sidecut (giving a large turning radius), they are poor freeriding boards.

BINDINGS

Bindings are designed as part of an integrated system of boots and board. Soft-boot bindings are used with freestyle boards and most freeriding boards. Plate bindings — for hard-shell boots, including ski boots — are used with some stiffer or longer freeriding boards, all freecarving boards, and all race boards.

FREESTYLE (2-BUCKLE) BINDINGS are soft-boot bindings made of high-strength resin or metal and come in different sizes. They have two micro-adjustable ratchet straps, which provide enough support for extreme

riding and enough flexibility for boned-out freestyle moves. They are available with either high or low backs. Low backs are designed to improve ankle flexibility for radical freestyle moves, but they *do* sacrifice heel-side performance. They are good for riders with very short boots and for riding a soft pipe.

BASELESS BINDINGS are just that: soft-boot bindings without a base. Your boot sits right on the deck of your board. Freestyle riders use base-less bindings to

get their boots as close to the snow as possible. This provides a better feel for the terrain, and in some cases allows for a more constant flexing of the board. One disadvantage of baseless bindings is that riders with large feet will get toe and heel overhang — what a drag! They also lack the adjustability of freestyle bindings (most have limited stance options), and many don't have adjustable forward lean. They are an acquired taste appreciated by the discerning few, so ride before you decide.

FREERIDE (3-BUCKLE) BINDINGS are the least common of all soft-boot bindings and are a three-buckle version of the freestyle binding. They offer adjustable flex and are ideal for all-terrain riding and heavy riders. This binding is the intermediate between freestyle and plate bindings for soft-boot riders.

PLATE BINDINGS are very similar to ski bindings and can only be used with hard boots. They are most commonly used with freecarve and race boards.

STEP-INS are the latest develoment in the boot-to-board interface and are here to stay. They're ideal for freeriding and allow for quick entry and exit without sitting. No more "wet butt"!

Their advantage is without question convenience. The downside to step-ins is that the support normally offered by the exo-skeleton structure of "classic" bindings has to be incorporated into the boot, which makes some boots too stiff for freestyle and others too soft for freeriding. The perfect combination of adjustability, support, flexibility,

and weight is still under development, but it is not far off.

INSERT PATTERNS

The almost-standard binding insert pattern is the 4X4, so named because the four inserts form a four-by-four centimeter square. Burton Snowboards uses a "3D" insert pattern on all their boards (except the baseless-binding model) but offers their bindings with both a 3D and 4X4 option. Both will be around for years to come.

CHAPTER 4

BOARD NEWS: THE TWIN-TIP, DIRECTIONAL BOARDS, AND DIRECTIONAL TWINS

The three most popular freeriding boards — the directional, the twin-tip, and the evolutionary directional twin — look very similar but have slightly different riding characteristics. If you want to know why boards are designed the way they are and which one is best for you, read on. (If you already know, good for you. Your gold star will be mailed to you shortly.)

DIRECTIONAL BOARDS are designed with a stiffer tail than nose section and perform best when ridden in one direction. Their camber and waist (point of maximum sidecut) are also set back of center. A directional board's stiff tail lets you ride with a stance back of center, which gives your board more float. It also gives you stability for jumping and landing tricks and pumping out of turns. These boards also tend to have a slightly deeper sidecut, in the form of a narrower waist, than twin tips.

(This may be a consideration for riders with big feet.)

Although directional boards are designed for the best of all-mountain riding, many models are ideal for freestyle and for riding the halfpipe, especially if the pipe is hard. In fact, many top pro-freestyle riders ride directional boards for freeriding and for competing in the pipe.

Directional boards perform well with a variety of stances, but perform at their best with a stance centered over their waist. In most cases, this is 1 to 1.5 inches back of center.

TWIN TIPS have identical nose and tail sections, a centered camber, sidecut,

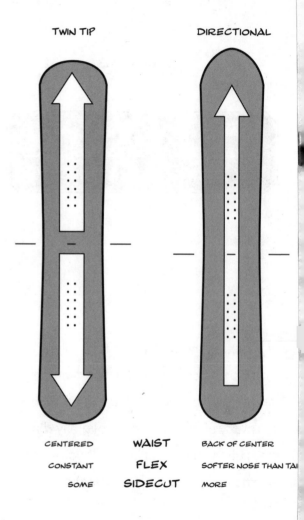

TWIN TIP	WAIST	DIRECTIONAL
CENTERED	WAIST	BACK OF CENTER
CONSTANT	FLEX	SOFTER NOSE THAN TAIL
SOME	SIDECUT	MORE

and stance, and have a constant flex pattern — they have no front or back. This design is ideal for riding fakie and doing switch tricks (backwards). Twin tips' flex patterns are normally softer and have less sidecut than directional boards of the same length. Twins are easy to ride, have a light feel, and are designed for pure freestyle. On the downside, their performance decreases at higher speeds and on icy terrain.

Because twin tips are designed to be ridden with a centered stance and have a softer flex pattern, they offer less float in powder than a freeriding board of the same length. This can be corrected by moving the stance back of center, but the only time you want to move your stance back of center on a twin tip is for powder.

The third (and newest) shape to grace the slopes is the **DIRECTIONAL TWIN**. It was developed by demanding pros who wanted the best of both the directional and twin shapes. (Bless those spoiled pros!) What they ended up with is almost a twin-tip shape, with a deeper sidecut that is centered or just back of center, and a stiffer tail. (Some models also have a slightly fuller nose shape for better performance in powder.) These boards offer better riding performance at speed and are ideal for switch riding and the pipe. Most pro-signature models on the market are a variant of a directional twin.

Directional twins are still a fairly new innovation and will continue to undergo minor refinements to sidecut and flex — but I believe they will become the standard.

AT-A-GLANCE PERFORMANCE CHART*

BOARD	CARVING	SPINNING	RIDING SWITCH	JUMPS	POWDER
Directional	Very Good	Good	Very Good	Very Good	Excellent
Twin Tip	Good	Excellent	Excellent	Very Good	Good
Directional Twins	Very Good	Very Good	Excellent	Very Good	Very Good

*The following rating scale is relative. Compare them to each other, not to absolutes.

CHAPTER 5

SPECIAL RIDER NEEDS: BIG BOYS, WOMEN, KIDS

TOYS FOR BIG BOYS

Most boards on the market today are designed and manufactured for specific groups of riders. There are boards for kids, women, and men. But there are few specifically designed for heavy riders —

over 85 kg. Many boards will still perform well for heavy riders, but not as well as they would for riders under 85 kg.

WEIGHT AND EFFECTIVE EDGE: Performance is a function of your weight-to-effective-edge ratio, and the board's sidecut and stiffness (see Chapter 2). My tests have shown (the hard way) that on a given board at a constant speed, heavier riders have less control on icy or hard-pack conditions, have less spring for airs, and less control on landings than lighter riders on the same board.

Many heavy riders have been compensating for the reduced performance of short freestyle boards by riding longer boards — 160 cm and longer — for the increased effective edge. If you don't mind riding a longer board, you don't have a problem. But if you're a big freestyler looking to spin some fresh tricks, a long board won't do. You need a short board for the reduced swing (spin) weight and maneuverability. Until recently, you had few options.

BOARDS: Many companies are producing freestyle boards that are "wide" or "fat" for riders with big feet (size 11 or larger). Many have sidecuts and flex patterns that are similar to their narrower cousins, but they may be a little less responsive.

CUSTOM BOARDS: If all else fails and nothing seems to work, you can get a custom freestyle or freeriding board made for you. Call one of the factories and place a special order, but be prepared to pay for it. That way you can ride a short, stiff board that will perform the way you want it to.

BOOTS: Use the stiffest soft boots available — even for freestyle. You can also use stiffer insoles in your boots. This will make your edge-to-edge transitions more responsive. Remember, bigger boots are not thicker, just bigger — which means that they are relatively softer than the same boots in a smaller size. If your feet are size 11 or larger, or if you weigh 85 kg or more, you should consider a stiff boot.

If soft boots still don't give you the support you need, try a hybrid or (gasp) hard boots.

BINDINGS: Some heavy riders find plastic bindings too soft and flexible. If this is you, try metal or carbon bindings; they're stiffer and stronger.

WOMEN

BOARDS: Women usually have smaller feet and weight less than men of the same height. As a result, boards made specially for women are softer and narrower for faster edge-to-edge transitions. Most major companies now offer boards for women, but some are just men's or kids' models with pretty graphics. Don't be fooled. Check the flex (it should be softer), the width (it should be narrower), and the length (it should be shorter) against a similar-style men's board before you decide if a women's board is right for you.

BOOTS: Women's boots have a narrow heel, a higher arch, and a lower cuff for a more comfortable fit and ride. Equipment is a personal thing, ride before you decide what's best for you.

KIDS

The kids' market is growing every year — with an estimated half of all new kids on the slopes riding snowboards. Every major manufacturer makes kids' equipment, some with the same exacting standards used for their pro models. These aren't little planks, they're boards that perform. That's why many may seem expensive! On the up-side, the re-sale market for kids' equipment is very strong.

CHAPTER 6

STANCE: IT ALL STARTS HERE

Choosing the right stance is as important as choosing the right board, regardless of how and where you ride. A solid, balanced riding style is impossible without a solid, balanced stance. Unless you fully understand the relationship between stance and performance, you want to read this chapter. It's amazing how small changes in stance width, binding angles, or boot centering have such a noticeable impact on riding performance.

I have listed, in order of importance, four things to consider when installing or adjusting your bindings.

BE CENTERED. The importance of being centered over the centerline of your board (from toe to heel) cannot be overstated. When you're centered, your board will perform the way it was designed to, and your turns will be faster, smoother, and more symmetrical.

With some soft boots, finding the centerpoint is not always obvious. Set your bindings across your board (zero degrees), adjust your toe and heel overhang, then rotate your bindings to the desired angles. If you wear a boot size smaller than a men's 6 or larger than a men's 10, check this adjustment closely.

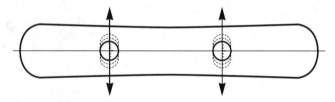

DETERMINE THE BEST STANCE WIDTH. Stance width will vary slightly with the kind of riding you want to do and the length of your board. As a starting point, use a comfortable shoulder-width stance; it should feel strong and stable. (Strap in on the carpet at home to check it out.) A wide stance will improve your balance and promote independent leg action, required for spinning

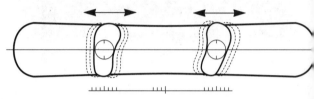

and jumping. But if your stance is too wide, your turns will suffer, because there is less effective edge in front of and behind your feet. And if your stance is unnaturally wide for your leg length, you risk injuring your knees.

DETERMINE YOUR STANCE ANGLES. Stance angles will vary with riding style, equipment, and conditions. The greater

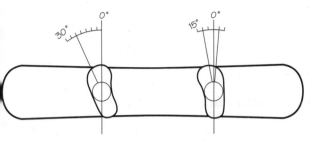

the sidecut of your board, the greater your stance angles should be to maximize the board's performance. As a starting point, try not to have more than a 15-degree difference between your front foot and back foot. This will improve your body alignment and let your hips rotate naturally when you ride. It may also reduce the risk of knee injury during a bad fall.

If you have large feet, you may have to increase your stance angles to eliminate or at least reduce toe and heel overhang. Another option is the duck stance; the choice of some top freestyle riders. Experiment until you find a stance that feels comfortable for your riding style.

INCREASE THE FORWARD LEAN ON YOUR BINDINGS. Increasing the forward lean on your highbacks will instantly improve your heel-side turns. Adjust your highbacks so that they fit snugly against the backs of your boots when you're standing up straight. By reducing any gaps between your boots and highbacks, you improve the initiation of the turn. If you leave a gap and you have to "hike out" to reach your highbacks, you are no longer balanced and ready to react to changes in terrain. It's a little adjustment that goes a long way.

CHANGE WITH THE TIMES

Your stance should be as versatile as you are. Adjust it to match the snow conditions and your riding style.

IN POWDER move your stance back of center to give your board more "float" (try one inch to start). If you ride a short twin-tip, you will notice a real difference. If you get a cramp in your front foot when riding powder, try increasing the angle on your front binding.

IN HARD-PACK CONDITIONS you may want to narrow your stance (start with one inch narrower) and increase your stance angles (try 25 degrees front and 10 degrees back) to give your board more effective edge and performance. If you're riding a centered stance on a twin-tip, move both bindings together. If you're riding a freeriding board, you can move them one at a time, starting with the back binding, then the front binding.

IN A HALFPIPE or in a snowboard park, reduce your binding angles, especially on the back foot. If you want to try a duck stance, get comfortable riding and spinning first before jumping. This stance is not for everyone.

Ride like the pros, carry a small screwdriver and change your stance often. It only takes a minute and it's well worth it.

STANCE: A QUICK REFERENCE

If you're having trouble getting all this straight, use this chart as a starting point, then adjust as described above for different snow conditions:

FOR FREESTYLE	STANCE WIDTH	ANGLES
140-150 cm board	18", 19", or 20"	Front 15° / Back 5°
150-160 cm board	19", 20", or 21"	Front 15° / Back 5°
FOR FREERIDING		
140-150 cm board	18", 19", or 20"	Front 25° / Back 15°
150-165 cm board	19", 20", or 21"	Front 25° / Back 15°

Leg length will determine stance width. For riders five-foot-four and shorter, try the smallest of the recommended stance widths. For tall riders, five-foot-ten or taller, try the largest of the recommended stance widths.

CHAPTER 7

HEEL LIFT: KEEP YOUR FEET ON THE GROUND

To ride with confidence and control, your feet must fit securely in your boots and bindings — without heel lift. Snowboard companies have paid their top pro riders and research-and-development teams big bucks to get their equipment just right. They have done their part, and now it's up to you to ride your equipment the way it was meant to be ridden. One indication that your bindings may need adjustment is heel lift. Here are several quick adjustments that will cure your heel-lift problems once and for all.

RAISE YOUR ANKLE STRAPS

Raising the anchor point of your bindings' ankle straps, so that they pull your heels to the back of your bindings at a 45-degree angle, will reduce or eliminate heel lift. This simple adjustment not only increases performance, you'll find it more comfortable.

A low ankle-strap anchor point is intended for use in the halfpipe, where

SYMPTOMS OF HEEL LIFT AND POSSIBLE ADJUSTMENTS

• HEEL LIFT ON TOE-SIDE TURNS AND LANDING JUMPS?
    RAISE ANKLE STRAPS.

• SORE ARCHES FROM TIGHT ANKLE STRAPS?
    RAISE AND LOOSEN ANKLE STRAPS.

• SORE ARCHES EVEN WITH STRAPS RAISED?
    BOOTS TOO SMALL FOR BINDINGS.

• PROBLEM INITIATING TOE-SIDE TURNS?
    BOOTS NOT CENTERED ON CENTERLINE OF BOARD.

• HEEL LIFT IN SOFT BOOTS ONLY?
    USE FOOTBEDS.

flexibility (a.k.a. "tweaking") is critical. The higher (standard) adjustment is designed for all-round freeriding and freestyle. It is the setting of choice with most pros, even in the pipe.

MOUNT YOUR BINDINGS ACROSS THE CENTERLINE OF THE BOARD

If you experience heel lift when initiating a toe-side turn, your boots may not be mounted over the centerline of the board. This is a critical adjustment and is often overlooked by shop technicians who install your bindings without your boots. If your bindings are mounted on the heel-side of your board's centerline, you have to apply extra pressure to your toe-side edge to initiate or complete your turn, causing your heels to lift. If you have small feet (size 5 to 7), check to make sure your bindings are centered on the centerline of your board.

TRY FOOTBEDS IN YOUR BOOTS

Footbeds are insoles you can buy with elevated heel cups and arches, and are a quick and inexpensive way to reduce or eliminate heel lift in your boots. Heel lift is a common problem for women and children who wear men's boots. Footbeds also make your boots warmer and more comfortable.

INCREASE THE FORWARD LEAN ON YOUR BINDINGS

By now you should know that increasing the forward lean on your highbacks improves your heel-side turns (see page 33 in the previous chapter). It also increases the "cradling" effect of the binding around your heel and ankle, and will make your toe-side turns more responsive and more comfortable. Adjust your highbacks so that they fit snugly against the backs of your boots when you're standing up straight. It's that easy.

TRY BOOTS WITH HEEL ANCHOR-STRAPS

Heel anchor-straps, also known as heel-lift kits, have been around for several years now, and are a standard feature on many freeriding boots. If you have a narrow ankle and suffer from heel lift, consider boots with these straps. They really work and offer an extra degree of adjustability.

SMALL FEET? TRY SMALL BINDINGS

The right combination of boots and bindings is important and often overlooked. If you have small boots (men's

SYMPTOMS OF HEEL LIFT AND POSSIBLE ADJUSTMENTS

- BOOTS AND BINDINGS MATCH, EVERYTHING MOUNTED RIGHT, BUT STILL SLIGHT HEEL LIFT?
  INCREASE FORWARD LEAN OF YOUR HIGHBACKS.

- STILL HAVE PROBLEMS?
  TRY CUSTOM-FIT FOOTBEDS.

- STILL HAVE PROBLEMS?
  TRY CUSTOM LINERS.

- STILL HAVE PROBLEMS? IT'S PROBABLY TECHNIQUE; TAKE A LESSON.

size 6 or smaller), be sure to ride with small bindings. A good binding is designed to cradle your boot evenly to prevent pressure points and heel lift. If your bindings are too big, your only support will be from the binding straps. To prevent heel lift, and to feel secure in your bindings, you will have to crank your straps down so tightly you could get foot cramps, cold feet, and even risk serious injury in a bad fall.

CHAPTER 8

DRESS THE PART

Snowboarding is an athletic activity, and you're sure to heat up. Wear layers that you can shed or vent if you get too warm. Your underwear is going to stay with you through thick and thin (or hot and cold) and should wick moisture away from your skin. Your insulating layer, like a fleece, is designed to keep you warm but not restrict mobility. Your shell, or outer layer, should be water- and wind-resistant and fit loosely. If you normally ride in cold climes, you may want to consider a jacket with a hood. Adjust or modify your layers to suit the conditions and the type of riding you do.

Like it or not, you will be spending time on your butt. If you're not wearing snowboarding pants, you may want to wear padded clothing (old hockey pants, padded in-line skating tights, etc.) or an extra pair of shorts over your underwear to add extra insulation – where it matters most.

Learn to snowboard when the snow is soft, but if you can't wait, consider wrist protectors (like the ones used by in-line skaters), knee-pads, and even a helmet. Not all snowboard schools offer these items, so you may want to bring your own.

GET A GRIP

The most critical clothing accessory for snowboarding is your handwear. Your mitts or gloves have to keep you warm and dry, allow you to adjust your bindings without having to take them off, and withstand the abrasion of a high-speed fall on hard snow or ice. Ski gloves and mitts are designed to be used with poles, and even the best ones won't do; they will disintegrate after just a few days of riding.

Snowboarding is a hands-on sport, so keep them warm and happy. Here's a summary of the important features:

WARMTH AND MOBILITY. Mitts are normally warmer than gloves with fingers but they offer less dexterity, and you will want to be able to adjust your bindings without removing your handwear. Pre-formed palms and articulated fingers (and thumbs) improve comfort and dexterity. To combine features of both mitts and gloves, companies offer the "lobster claw" or "trigger finger" (a three-finger mitt).

You can also ride with a mitt outer-shell over a glove liner — the best of both worlds. And be sure not to buy either gloves or mitts too big.

Try wearing **RESILIANT MATERIALS** like Kevlar, nylon, and synthetic leathers. They withstand the abrasion of ice and hard snow and the sharp edges of your board — and they're water resistant.

PULL-OUT OR CHANGEABLE LINERS let you change your liners to suit the weather conditions, and they dry faster. They are highly recommended.

HIGH CUFFS with quick-cinch wrist straps keep snow out and are a standard feature on most gloves and mitts. These straps should also quick-release with only one hand.

SUPPORT. Some gloves have built-in wrist protectors to help prevent sprains or breaks. Most mitts are large enough to accommodate wrist protectors over your liners.

SEE NO EVIL: GOGGLES FOR EVERYONE!

Goggles are the preferred eyewear of snowboarders. They offer great

> "NOTHING WILL KEEP YOU DRY IF YOU RIDE IN THE SPRING OR SUMMER ON A GLACIER. IF KEEPING WARM IS NOT A CONSIDERATION, WEAR RUBBERIZED GARDENING GLOVES; THEY'RE DRY, RUGGED, AND COST ONLY FOUR BUCKS!"

protection from harmful ultra-violet rays, reduce glare, are warmer than sunglasses, and don't fall off.

Your goggles go where you go. If you're spinning tricks or lofting cliffs, you've got to have them. If you're riding in the trees, you need them — you never know when a stray branch will cross your path. If you're not a fair-weather rider (and you won't be), you need them for warmth. If you ride in sunny conditions, you've got to have them — the glare off the snow is 25 times more intense than the light in an office building. You don't want snowblindness.

All goggles stay clear because they are vented. Venting is good, but too much can dry your eyes and give you an ice-cream headache — especially in cold conditions. Too little venting, and your goggles will fog at slower speeds or when you are hiking. Goggles' performance depends on the fit, your riding style, and weather conditions. It really is a personal thing. Since goggles demos are uncommon (at least for now), borrow your friends' before you decide.

It goes without saying that you only get what you pay for. When it comes to your eyes, don't compromise.

CHAPTER 9

GETTING STARTED: IT'S ONLY AS HARD AS THE SNOW!

There are two laws you must always remember when snowboarding:

1) snowboarding should always be fun; and

2) snowboarding is only as hard as the snow.

Keep this in mind and the rest is easy.

The checklist below is the minimum you should demand from your first snowboarding experience and should carry you over the threshold in a big way.

STANCE, WIDTH, AND ANGLES

If you've never surfed, ridden a skateboard or a wakeboard, or ridden a slalom water ski, you probably think "regular" is a gasoline and "goofy" is a Disney thing. Wrong! If you ride with your left foot forward, you ride regular; and if you ride with your right foot forward, you ride goofy (it comes from surfing). It doesn't matter which way you ride as long as you put your best foot forward. If you don't know, ask your instructor to help you decide. He or she will probably give you a little push (or pull) to help you figure it out. If you still aren't sure, try both ways and go with what feels the most natural. Only about 20 per cent of all riders ride goofy, and most of them are left-handed. If nothing feels natural — and you aren't left-handed — try the regular stance a little longer.

Your stance should be almost shoulder-width and feel strong (as if you were preparing to pick up a big bag of potatoes), and you should feel no pressure in your knees. For stance angles, I recommend 25 degrees for the front and 15 for the back as a starting point. (For more detailed information on stance options, see Chapter 6.)

BOARDS

If you're renting, you want to rent a freeriding board, and make sure it's not too short. You need a board that has a long-enough effective edge to support your weight and give you control when turning and stopping.

Here's what I recommend:

Your weight	Length of Board*
up to 130 lbs	140 cms
130-145 lbs	150 cms
150-165 lbs	155 cms
165 + lbs	160 cms

*applicable for freeriding or freestyle boards

HARD OR SOFT BOOTS?

I recommend soft boots for your first lesson (even if you're an expert skier), because they are more comfortable and forgiving for learning than hard shells or ski boots and you won't fall as much. Once you have experimented with the basics (this should take about two hours), then you can step into hard boots and plates — if you still want to.

BACK TO SCHOOL

Without question, the best way to get started is to take a lesson. Every reputable ski school offers certified

instructors. Remember snowboarding's first law? Well, you may forget it during your first few hours on a snowboard. Don't get discouraged, and set realistic goals for yourself. Snowboarding has a very steep learning curve, so if you make it to day two, the first law becomes impossible to forget.

Now get out there and let the fun begin! The only regret you'll have is that you didn't start sooner.

CHAIRLIFTS FOR BEGINNERS

Riding a chairlift is as easy as riding the bus: you get on, you gab with your neighbor, then you get off.

GETTING ON THE BUS:

• If you ride regular, get on the right side of the chair; if you ride goofy, get on the left side of the chair. (This really helps, and you'll see why later.)

• Face the chair from your toe-side and reach for the chair with your back hand. Sit when ready.

Don't let the chair slam into the back of your legs. Bring the footrest down, and relax.

• Start gabbing!

GETTING OFF THE BUS:

• When you get to your stop, raise the footrest and prepare to stand up.

• As your board touches the snow, wedge your back foot against your back binding for support, then stand up.

(Be sure to have a stomp or non-skid pad on your board.) A little toe overhang is good.

• Push off the chair with your back hand. This will help you get into position.
• Now relax, keep your weight low, and apply pressure to your toe-side edge to turn and stop. Because you're on the end of the chair, no one is in your way. (Told ya it would help!)

If you still have problems getting off the chair, climb a slope that resembles the outrun of the chairlift, and practice once or twice. Ride out with your back foot against your back binding and turn to your toe-side.

RIDING A T-BAR

T-bars are an embarrassing reminder of a pre-snowboarding world. Because of our sideways, one-foot-out stance, it's a lot harder going up than it is going down. T-bars are still a reality at many small centers and on some glaciers, so you might as well learn how to deal with them. Here are some tips that may help:

• Watch others to get a feel for timing and your placement.

• Ride solo on your first few attempts.

• Get into position. Face the bar with your board pointing uphill. Many riders like to place their back foot on the snow for balance. (If you ride regular, facing uphill you will be on the left side of the bar, and if you ride goofy, you will be on the right side of the bar.)

• Grab the bar from the liftie with two hands. You have the option of placing the tee under your butt or between your thighs.

•   Anchor your back foot against the back binding before you start moving.

• Place one hand on the tee to stabilize it.

• Keep your weight centered evenly over both feet and let the tee pull you. Don't sit on the tee

CHAPTER 10

BASIC TECHNIQUES

It's impossible to tell you in a book all there is to know about snowboarding technique. What I can share, however, is what I (and a team of experts) consider to be the unchanging fundamentals of snowboarding. The principles behind these techniques repeat themselves in all kinds of riding – from racing, to the halfpipe – and will serve you well, regardless of your riding style or ability.

STAY CENTERED

In Chapter 6, I stressed the importance of having a stance that's centered over the waist and across the centerline of your board.

The length of a board's effective edge is related to the board's flex pattern, stiffness, and sidecut. When your weight is evenly distributed over your stance, your board will flex evenly, and the pressure on your edges is evenly distributed. This is how snowboards were designed to be ridden — regardless of riding style or terrain. Riding centered will not only increase control, but it will also let you make smooth, symmetrical turns and let you quickly adjust to changing terrain.

This equipment-centered approach to snowboarding is taught only in high-end snowboarding schools and camps — it is not yet the norm. Ironically, difficulties in learning to snowboard have more to do with improper equipment set-up than with poor technique. The proper equipment, adjusted for your height, weight, and foot size, is the best start to snowboarding that you can get.

THE TEST: If you find yourself sliding out on your heel-side turns or spearing the nose of your board into soft snow or moguls, you may be putting too much weight on your front leg. This is especially common with skiers who are learning to snowboard. To fix the problem, concentrate on applying equal pressure to both feet in your turns.

If you ride fakie (leading with your back leg) or have tried spinning your board, you will quickly learn that keeping your weight centered is not only a fundamental principle of snowboarding, it's a fundamental principle of survival. If you don't stay centered, the results can be eye opening.

Most snowboards are designed by riders who know how to get the most performance from the shortest board. This gives them both control and maneuverability. When you ride, do the same — by staying centered.

THE TWIST: The twist of the upper body to face the direction of travel is a North American quirk and has its roots in skiing. The rationale is that by facing the direction of travel, you can better prepare for changes in terrain and are positioned halfway between a heel-side and a toe-side turn.

There is no question that beginners find their heel-side turns more controlled when their upper body is turned to face the direction of travel. But this has more to do with being centered than with twisting the torso.

The Euros proved this in a big way. Many of the top riders from Europe and Scandinavia ride with a fully square (but centered) stance — with no twist in the upper body. This technique lets them ride switch and prepare for airs with minimum weight transfer. The square stance has proven itself on the World Cup circuit, and is rapidly becoming the standard for freestyle riders.

It really doesn't matter how you ride, as long as you ride. And if you ride centered, your board will perform to its potential — which will keep you grinning — and that's what snowboarding is all about!

UP, OVER, AND DOWN

All snowboarding maneuvers can be described in three phases: an extension, a transition, and a compression.

The **extension** phase occurs when you extend your body (away from the snow) to unweight the pressure of your board on the snow. The more you extend, the less pressure on your edge and the less control you have.

The **transition** phase occurs at the point of maximum extension, when you transit from one edge to the other (from toe to heel or vice versa). The transition is the shortest of the three phases and is the one of least control.

The **compression** phase is when you weight your board to apply pressure to the new edge. The point of maximum compression is when your board is fully flexed and will deliver the most turning performance.

RHYTHM

The extension and compression phases of your turns should be equal. (The time spent weighting and unweighting your edge in a turn should be the same.) This is known as rhythm. Good riders always ride with rhythm — even if it's very subtle. They never ride their boards flat. A flat board is unresponsive and is more likely to catch an edge than a board that is flexing.

SYMMETRY

Your turns have symmetry when the arcs of your toe-side and heel-side turns are equal. When they are, your extension and compression phases are equal, and the pressure you apply throughout to your edges (by compressing) is also equal. A good way to give yourself feedback on your turns is to make some symmetrical turns under a chairlift in fresh snow, then study them on the way up. If your heel-side turns differ from your toe-side turns, adjust your compression and extension accordingly.

If you're wondering how these basic principles of snowboarding apply to powder, freeriding, and freestyle, you're on the ball. The length of the phase and the amount of pressure applied to your edge will change depending on the type of riding you do, but the phases themselves are always there.

In freestyle, for example, an exaggerated extension will get you airborne, and the transition will be in the form of an air, a spin, or a combination of both.

In racing and performance carving, the extension phase of your turn is subtle and the emphasis is on the compression phase, for control at high speeds. When racing gates, the compression phase will also start and finish sooner than it does in freecarving.

In powder, the extension phase of your turn (the one that gives your board float) is the most critical. The transition phase involves no edge pressure and the compression phase is subtle.

In freestyle, all the phases are important: the extension is exaggerated to prepare for airs and spins; the transition phase is where you do spins or grabs; and the compression is where you touch down and control is regained. All the phases are still there, it's just that they get more complicated.

CHAPTER 11

TERRAIN AWARENES: THE LINE LESS TRAVELED

Prerequisite: a snowboard
Degree of difficulty: rider's choice

Whether you're riding a steep powder-bowl or a gentle, groomed slope, your fun shouldn't be limited by the terrain you ride. A good freerider makes the most of each run, constantly seeking out new challenges and means of expression. Regardless of how long you've been riding, you can learn to optimize your snowboarding experience. You can learn to ride the line less traveled.

ANTICIPATE CHANGING TERRAIN

A mountain's terrain changes constantly, and to expand your horizons, you have to anticipate the changes. If you see a lip, or hit, in the distance, adjust your line to get you there. If you anticipate ice, moguls, or crowds, you may want to ride the soft snow on the shoulder of the run. If you see a flat

section ahead, maintain enough speed to carry you across — and for fun, ride it switch. Bored? Try exploring the side of runs, where soft snow and jumps await. The days of riding down the middle of a run are over — don't even think of going there again. By adapting to changing snow conditions and terrain, you will always be in control. What follows are different kinds of terrain and some ways to make the most of them. (Moguls are covered in Chapter 15.)

FLATS

Flats don't have to be boring. They're a great place to practice spinning tricks and riding fakie (see Chapter 12). If you're new to these tricks, try them at slow speeds, traveling across the slope, and be sure to practice your spins in both directions (frontside and backside). Flats almost always have hits where you can practice small airs and spins. Once you've mastered your spins on the ground, you're ready to try them in the air, and the flats are a great place to start.

Remember, you don't have poles, so maintain enough speed to get you to where you are going. And keep your board waxed, it really helps!

MODERATE TERRAIN

Not too flat, not too steep – just perfect for mixing up short- and long-radius turns. The harder the snow, the more you compress and set your edge. Keep your speed up, get a rhythm going, and pull some "Gs." Let the wind blow through your hair, it's great therapy.

If you're an advanced rider, airs and carving switch with speed are your next challenge. No guts, no glory.

STEEP TERRAIN

When talking terrain, steep is a relative thing; control is for real. Control your speed by compressing hard and using your edges to slow you down. Don't be intimidated; instead, be aggressive and exaggerate your movements and set your edge with confidence. Steep pitches can get icy and bare. Pick a line where the snow has accumulated or spot lone patches of soft snow and turn on them. Nothing sucks the life out of a run more than ice, so avoid it. (Ice is for hockey and drinks.)

Riding steep terrain is a great way to push your limits (and your heart rate), just don't compromise safety.

The snow conditions will dictate how far out of the envelope you can ride. Fresh snow is the best, but it's scarce in most commercial ski/snowboard centers, so you may have to improvise. If you're like most riders, your heel-side turn is weaker than your toe-side turn, so pick a line where your heel-side turn is on the shoulder of the run, where soft snow accumulates. (Regular riders will ride down the right side of the run, and goofy-foot riders down the left.)

The next time you're out riding, don't just ride, maximize the terrain. Try not to ride the same run the same way all day. Ride switch, mix up short- and long-radius turns, add spins and airs; it's what snowboarding is all about.

CHAPTER 12

RIDING FAKIE: PULL THE SWITCH

Riding fakie is not only for top freestyle riders, it's a basic staple of snowboarding. Without it, you're not a complete rider! A true all-terrain vehicle has to work in reverse. (Besides, it really separates us from skiers. Okay, buddy, let's see you land a 540!)

FAKIE AND SWITCH

One of the many great things about snowboarding is being able to do everything forwards (or nose fist) and backwards (or tail first). If you're riding backwards, you're riding fakie (an expression borrowed from the skateboard world). If you initiated a trick tail first, you did the trick switch. (I just wanted to clear that up!)

Riding fakie is a great way to develop a feel for your board and to hone your balance. It can also add challenge to an otherwise boring run and is a great way to rest a tired front leg!

STARTING OUT

The prerequisite to riding fakie is knowing how to spin a 180 on the snow. This ensures you a safe "out" if you get into trouble — and at first you will. Riding fakie is best learned on a freestyle or freeriding board with soft boots. (Carving alpine boards fakie is an advanced maneuver.) Mount your bindings in the center of twin-tip boards and an inch back of center on directional boards. To start, try stance angles of 15 to 25 degrees on the front and 5 to 10 degrees on the back. Pick a gentle slope that isn't too busy, and fake it till you make it. At first, it will be easier to traverse the slope and to slide your turns (extend instead of compress in the turn).

INTERMEDIATE RIDERS

As you get more comfortable riding fakie, increase your speed, decrease your turning radius, and start carving your turns (compressing in the turns). Practice your noserolls and tailrolls and get them down pat. They're a great way to get into and out of switch tricks. Now venture out into new terrain. It's important to be able to ride powder, moderately steep terrain, and absorb small bumps, all ass-first.

ADVANCED RIDERS

The best snowboarders are strong switch riders. (Good trivia: Two-time world freestyle champion Terje Haakonsen of Norway has competed in boardercross-style races riding fakie and still won!) Many riders who normally ride small hills maximize the terrain by learning their tricks switch (then they move to ski resorts to show them off).

The best way to land fakie is to do a frontside 180. Start off small to build up your control and confidence. Once comfortable landing fakie, try taking off fakie — this would be your first switch air! Now do a switch air grab (big style points) and you've earned (big) bragging rights.

HARD CORE

If you want to be a totally bi-directional rider, you are going to have to make the commitment. To get there, switch (pun intended) your bindings, and ride "the other way" for as long as it takes. You can also ride with a duck stance, and make sure you spend equal time riding regular and fakie.

Just imagine being able to ride, jump, and land tricks equally well forwards and backwards — the possibilities are endless. And as easy as it looks, I can assure you, it's more fun than it looks.

CHAPTER 13

POWDER

Your snowboarding quest ends with powder. The steeper and deeper the better. Mere words don't do justice to the nirvana of a true powder experience (and it just takes one). Like your first love or your first car, it's a significant emotional event you will never forget.

Most who have lived it will agree: riding powder is the heart and soul of snowboarding. It's what snowboards were designed for. Unlike skiing, where the deeper the snow, the more demanding the technique, snowboarding in powder is only as hard as the snow.

But as easy as it is, a few good tips can never hurt.

TECHNIQUES FOR THE NEWLY CHRISTENED: The deeper the snow, the more you will have to exaggerate the extension and compression of your turns. With a little practice, you will develop a subtle bounce underfoot, which will make for a more dynamic turn — you know, the frozen-smoke hero-turns that dreams are made of. Edges are completely redundant in powder, so don't even think of using them.

STANCE: If it's not broken, don't fix it. But if your board is short and needs a little more "float," try moving your stance 1 to 1.5 inches back of center.

STANCE ANGLES: If you ride with small binding angles and don't plan on riding fakie in the powder, you may want to increase your binding angles — especially on your front foot. This will reduce foot pressure and leg fatigue.

BOARDS: Always ride whatever board you're most comfortable with. But if the snow is very deep or heavy, and it's not as much fun as I make it sound, try a board that's 5 to 10 cm longer than what you normally ride.

WARNING! Riding powder is totally addictive. So much so, that heli- and cat-boarding operations are all reporting rapid growth. A fringe element of snowboarders are also using snowmobiles to seek out pristine pastures of white gold. For others, backcountry hiking is the purest and most gratifying way to get their fix (see Chapter 16). Any way you find it, when you do, you may never be the same again.

CHAPTER 14

GETTING AIR

This chapter is for all riders.

Prerequisite: the thirst for adventure.
Degree of difficulty: basic to expert.

Airs are a pure adrenaline rush, and are as much a part of snowboarding as riding switch and hunting down powder. Regardless of what the ski-patrols will tell you, jumping is unavoidable. Airs are a form of expression unmatched in any other sport and are part of the snowboard culture.

If you haven't started jumping yet, you will. It's as natural as riding over a crest with speed and floating until you touch down and ride away. The techniques for basic airs do not change as you get better – you just keep going fatter (see Glossary) and add more spins.

When first learning airs, don't worry about height, distance, or spinning. You should feel comfortable riding and be ready to push your limits. Safe airs are intentional and controlled.

PRE-FLIGHT CHECK

Jumps (also known as hits) come in all shapes and sizes and may not be immediately visible to the untrained eye. Follow riders of comparable ability who are getting air. This way, you will get a feel for the lines they ride and how they approach the hits. Look for gentle slopes where you can see the landing area, and approach them straight-on or across the fallline on your toe edge. Let your sense of adventure be your guide; half the fun is finding the hits.

Nice tuat shot

PREPARE FOR LIFTOFF

Approach the hit at a comfortable speed with a solid stance. Your knees and ankles should be slightly bent, and your weight should be balanced over your feet. Your arms should be relaxed and slightly in front of you. Don't bend at the waist!

LIFTOFF

The key to a controlled liftoff is to pop — by extending your legs and raising your arms — at the top of the hit. Timing is everything. The more you pop, the more air you will get. If things don't feel just right on the approach, absorb the hit and ride over it.

Be careful not to pop too aggressively or you could throw yourself off balance and end up rolling up the windows (a panic-induced circling of the arms to regain balance)!

LANDING- GEAR UP

Once in the air, bring your board up under you by bending your knees towards your chest. This will help keep you balanced and controlled in the air.

GEAR LOCKED

When you feel you can, grab your board – any grab will do, but many consider the Indy grab easiest. The Indy (where you grab your board on the toe edge with your back hand) is not only stylish, but it stabilizes your board in flight. (The grab has its roots in skateboarding, where the board is not attached to your feet.)

LANDING-GEAR DOWN

Spot your landing and extend your board to meet the snow before gravity gets you there. This lets you ease into the landing and adjust your stance (and balance) for the terrain. Maintain a strong stance and absorb the landing by compressing.

Believe it or not, a steep landing is best — even for beginners. Try to avoid flat landings; they're just too hard on the body. In fact, flat landings are responsible for most knee injuries in snowboarding.

I can't over-emphasize the importance of the "gear-up, gear-down" phases. They're the details that separate poetic, controlled flight from airborne human projectiles.

Getting air is an exhilarator like few others. It will keep your heart pumping and your eyes glowing.

Chapter 15

MOGULS

If you've experienced death by moguls, don't feel bad, many have fallen before you. They're not everyone's passion, and sometimes can't be avoided. But then again, moguls are just snow, and no snow is bad snow, right?

An effective technique for dealing with moguls is to square your shoulders to the fallline and keep your weight balanced over your stance. Your line and rhythm are everything. Keep your board turning and your legs pumping – even between moguls. Choose a line that's within your skill level; a line near the side of the run, where the moguls are smaller and less frequent, will be easier than a line in the center of the run.

You can use moguls to control your speed on a steep run. Traverse from mogul to mogul and initiate your turn on the way up, absorbing heavily and completing your turn on the way down. By working your front and back legs independently – like dual shock-absorbers – you will increase your balance and control.

Moguls make lovely jumps. If you get air, be sure it's intentional and not because you were sitting back. (If you sit back in the moguls, you will quickly know it.)

Shorter, softer boards are easier to control in moguls, but with the right technique, anything works — and works well. I've seen world-cup racers, riding long race-boards, blaze by expert skiers in the moguls, so I know anything is possible.

The best time to ride moguls is in the spring when they're soft and forgiving. Get out there and surprise yourself!

Chapter 16

RIDING THE BACKCOUNTRY: TIPS FOR A ONE-DAY HIKE

The quest for powder will make us do strange things. To find fresh snow, avoid crowds, lift-lines, and lift-tickets, many riders are venturing off-piste and into the backcountry for their snowboarding adventures. It's not only for the accomplished snowboarder, it's for the purist, the addict, and the adventurer — regardless of ability. There are some guidelines you should follow, however, before you grab your board, stuff your pack, and march off into the sunset.

The following section is designed as a guide for riders who want to experience the serenity of an off-piste hike and the exhilaration of a pristine descent. It contains the minimum you need to know.

PACK LIGHT

The bigger the pack, the greater the tendency to fill it. The trick is to bring as little as possible without bringing *too* little. Remember, you're a snowboarder, not a Sherpa guide.

Make sure your pack is comfortable, with your board securely strapped high and away from your body. There is nothing worse than your board moving about and hitting your calves as you hike. If you've never ridden with a pack, it's a good idea to get a feel for riding with one before your trek. Be sure your pack is secure; a pendulous pack will send you over-the-bars in soft snow before you know it.

BEFORE THE HIKE

• Tell your friends where you're going, including your exact departure time and estimated time of return.
• Collect as much information on your destination as possible.

• Determine the avalanche risk (if applicable).
• Check the weather forecast for the day of the hike and the day after the hike.
• Team up with riders of equal ability and with similar goals for the trek. This is more important than it sounds. You don't want to get separated because your buddy wants to ride a different line.

CHECKLIST: ONE PERSON, ONE KIT!

• Water (at least one liter), or water-purification tablets or a small water-purification kit.
• Food. Go big on the carbohydrates, such as pasta, and leave the sugar pops

at home. Pack trail mix and energy bars, such as PowerBars, PowerGel, or Cliff bars; you don't want a candy or diet bar here. Always pack for an extra day!

• Quality eyewear. Remember, the glare reflected off snow is 25 times that in the home or office.

• Extra clothes including socks, hat, gloves or mitts, T-shirts, and a shell.

• Spare laces (good for anything), and insert screws and a small screwdriver. If you're hiking the Rockies or the Coastal Mountains, bring a transceiver, which will signal your location if you're lost or buried under a slide. If you're hiking smaller mountains where slides are even a slight risk, bring a transceiver. It's a good idea to practice using them before you start your hike; in a slide, every second is precious. It's better to err on the side of caution.

Now fit all that into your day pack and make sure it weighs less than 5 per cent of your body weight. Within your group, you should also have:

• A first-aid kit.

• At least 20 feet of climbing rope.

• A small shovel for making hits and digging (just for fun).

ONE STEP AT A TIME

If you need snowshoes, use a modified bearpaw (an elongated model) with aluminum frames. They're light and offer good traction and floatation. (Don't forget you're heavier now with your pack.) If you're only hiking on snow, you can wear your snowboarding boots. If you're going out in the spring through varied terrain, it's better to wear hiking boots for added support and traction.

SAFETY FIRST

Always spot your terrain on the hike up. Occasionally check snow depth and layers for potential slides or buried rocks. If you're following a buddy, stay a minimum of 30 feet apart, just in case.

If on the way down you trigger a small slide, don't panic. Keep your speed up and ride it out diagonally to the slide. If you feel snow wrapping around your ankles, you're riding too slowly!

LEAVE YOUR LITTLE TWIN-TIP AT HOME

Backcountry riding is not a freestyle session. On the steeps, in the deeps, and with the added weight of a pack, you need a longer board for floatation and control. All mountain or extreme boards, between 160 and 175 cm (women, this also applies to you), are ideal for backcountry riding.

DRESS FOR SUCCESS

There is a saying in the backcountry:

"If you don't like the weather, wait five minutes." Dress appropriately. Layering works best, with thin polypropylene underwear, an insulating layer (like a fleece) then a waterproof shell. Avoid overheating whenever possible.

PICK YOUR OWN LINES

Study the terrain and choose your lines appropriately. Don't follow a sucker line — you could end up going off a cliff.

ONE LAST THING

Never underestimate Murphy's Law.

CHAPTER 17

THE FIVE-MINUTE TUNE-UP

Degree of difficulty (0-5): 1.5
Time required: 5 minutes

Does tuning your board make a noticeable difference? Yes it does! Sharp edges and a waxed base help you crank out turns like a racer (without the spandex), improve your edge-to-edge transitions, and glide across those annoying flats with ease. Waxing your board also makes your base harder and more resistant to damage — for when you ride on everything but snow.

Here are a few easy-to-follow steps that will help you keep your sharp edge. All you need is a side-edge filing tool for skis or snowboards, a fine flat file, wax remover, and any sort of iron. (I still use an old wonder-glide garage-sale special.)

Tuning your board can take as little as five minutes and will yield immediate returns.

• IF YOU FIND YOUR BASE HAS A BEVEL IN IT (A HIGH SPOT IN THE MIDDLE) YOU MAY WANT TO GET A "BASE GRIND." MANY SKI AND SNOWBOARD SERVICE CENTERS OFFER THIS FOR BETWEEN $15 AND $20. WHEN GETTING A BASE GRIND, REMOVE YOUR BINDINGS AND ASK FOR ONLY THE BASE TO BE GROUND, NOT THE SIDE EDGES. IN MY EXPERIENCE, SOME TECHNICIANS, IN A QUEST FOR PERFEC-TION, TAKE TOO MUCH EDGE OFF WITH THEIR MECHANICAL GRINDERS. (ONCE IT'S GONE, IT DOESN'T GROW BACK!) YOU CAN BETTER CON-TROL THE AMOUNT OF

(CONT'D ON PAGE 81)

1. Clean any dirt, oil, or old wax from your base with wax remover. If you don't, your file will gum up. If you don't have wax remover, you can use a petroleum-based thinner such as Varsol. Note, however, that Varsol and other thinners tend to dry out your base, so be sure to re-wax your board once you're finished sharpening your edges.

2. Start by filing the side-wall edge. (There's a reason for this, but it's too complex to explain here.) Use smooth, even strokes, applying pressure in only one direction. It doesn't matter which direction, just be consistent. (On a race board it matters, but not for freeriding.)

It's important to apply thumb pressure on the board to keep the file flat and against the edge. Use a 90-degree-angle setting on your side-edge tool. (Many alpine riders prefer to sharpen their edges at 88 degrees for more bite in icy conditions.)

3. When you have finished with both side-wall edges, take the file out of your side-edge sharpening tool for use on the base edge. (It works great on the side edges, so why wouldn't it work on the base edge?) Most files have a rough-cut side and a smooth or finishing cut on the flip side.

If your edges are in rough shape, start with the rough cut, then use the finishing cut.

Hold the file at about a 30-degree angle to the edge, and apply constant pressure to the file with your thumb to keep it flat on the board. Rest your forefinger (under the file) against the sidewall of your board to act as a guide. It's important to keep the file flat on the base of your board at all times. You want to sharpen your edges, not round them.

4. You should see little metal fillings in your file and on your board. This is good! Clean them off as you go.

5. Wax your board by melting the wax on your iron and letting it drip onto the board. If your wax smokes when you melt it, your iron is too hot. Run a bead of wax up and down each edge of your board, then, using the iron, smooth it into your base with a circular motion. Pay particular attention to working in the wax along the edges; these are the high-wear areas. Let the wax cool, then scrape it off with a wide scraper. (Plastic scrapers work as well as any, and are the cheapest.)

6. Go riding. You've just saved big bucks, so treat yourself.

(FROM PAGE 80)
EDGE YOU REMOVE WITH A FILE. IF YOUR EDGES ARE A MESS AND YOU NEED REAL HELP, TRY A COARSER FILE.

• IF YOU DON'T KNOW IF YOU'RE ACTUALLY FILING YOUR EDGE OR JUST SCRAPING P-TEX, COLOR YOUR EDGES WITH A BLACK MARKER. THIS WILL LET YOU SEE WHERE THE FILE IS BITING YOUR EDGE.

• YOU SHOULD NOT NEED MORE THAN ONE BASE GRIND PER SEASON.

• ALL WAXES WORK WELL, BUT THE MORE-EXPENSIVE WAXES ARE EASIER TO APPLY AND LAST LONGER.

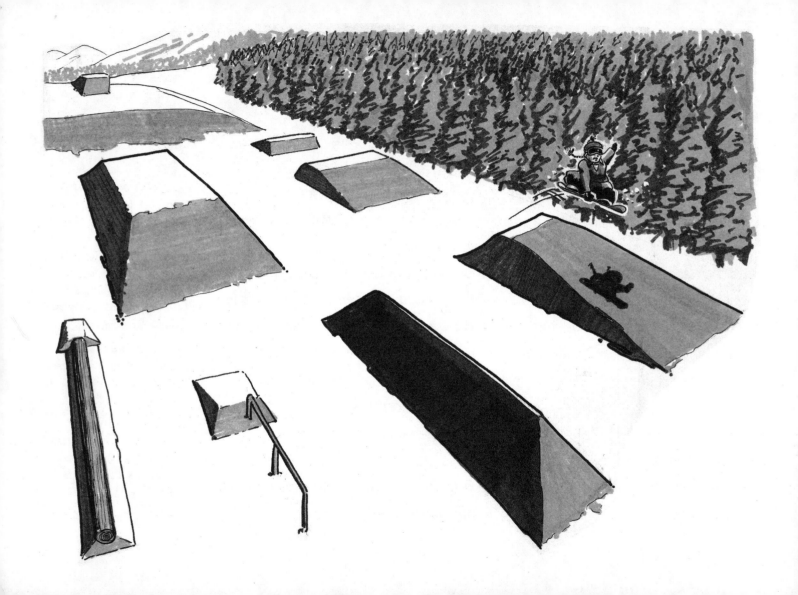

CHAPTER 18

SNOWBOARD PARKS: HOW TO MAKE THE MOST OF THEM

Snowboard parks, terrain parks, and fun parks are great places to hang out with like-minded adrenaline junkies and practice freestyle tricks. These parks are not just for young males with a high threshold for pain, most have something for everyone.

WHEN TO USE THE PARK

Never ride an icy park; it just isn't worth it. Go find some powder in the trees and save your butt for another day. In the winter, try to ride the park just after it has been groomed. Avoid riding it at the end of the day, when all the snow has been scraped off the landing areas. In the spring, ride the park in the late morning or the afternoon, when the snow softens.

REMEMBER: freestyle is only as hard as the snow.

HOW TO USE THE PARK

• Always study the take-off and landing areas of a jump before taking it.

- Try to start from the same spot each time to gauge your speed.
- Practice straight airs off a jump before attempting rotational airs.
- Work a jump or an obstacle until you can land several tricks comfortably. Then move on.
- Stay clear of landing areas and blind spots.
- Announce your intent to jump by calling "Dropping in" or "Next" before you go.
- Practice where you feel comfortable, and don't feel intimidated by hot riders and pros. (They, too, had humble beginnings.) Parks are for having fun!

CHAPTER 19

COMPETITIONS

man I have a tight ass

Snowboard competitions continue to play a significant role in the evolution of the sport. These contests are the focal point of the snowboard culture and are the proving grounds for the young stars of tomorrow. Many are made-for-media events that offer lucrative prizes and instant-hero status. New events continue to be developed as the sport of snowboarding evolves. What follows are some of the most popular events — at least for now.

THE HALFPIPE

The halfpipe was snowboarding's first competitive freestyle event, and has its origins in skateboarding. Competitors "drop in" and perform non-rotational airs, rotational airs, and inverted tricks, and are judged on degree of difficulty, control, and originality. It has been the showcase freestyle event since the early days of the sport, and, along with Super-G racing, has been chosen as an Olympic event. (See the complete halfpipe scoring system beginning on page 91.)

BOARDERCROSS

The boardercross (a.k.a. boarder-X) event is based on a motorcycle "motorcross," where four, six, or eight competitors race each other through an obstacle-filled course. The top half from each heat advances to the next round, saving the best for last. Banked turns, wave jumps, flats, and gaps make this event both technically challenging and exciting for spectators — especially when there's elbowing in the corners.

There is a variant of the boardercross, called the banked slalom — or, in the case of the U.S. Open, the Citizen Slingshot — that is also gaining popularity. The course for the banked slalom is very similar to a boardercross course (it may be slightly longer), but competitors race one at a time against the clock, not against each other. The advantage of this is that the best riders can't be accidently eliminated as a result of a collision or a pile-up in a corner. A properly designed course will favor neither hard nor soft-boot riders, and will be

won on ability, not the most expensive equipment.

Boardercross and banked slalom events are a pure form of snowboard competition, and because they are accessible to all riders, they will continue to gain popularity.

SLOPESTYLE

A slopestyle event is an on-snow version of the skateboard-park event where competitors ride through the park and are free to choose their terrain and their tricks. They are judged much as they are in the halfpipe event, except with more emphasis on variety and continuity. This event is popular with the new breed of riders, because competitors can perform a greater variety of tricks in a park than they can in a halfpipe. It showcases more of their all-mountain freestyle talents.

BIG AIR

The big air event is one of snowboarding's most spectacular freestyle events. As its name suggests, competitors perform big airs off big jumps — often for big cash prizes. They are judged for degree of difficulty, height, style, and control. These events are for experts only, and competitors must normally pre-qualify or be invited to participate.

EXTREME

These contests are backcountry down-hill events, where the chosen few challenge Mother Nature's extremes. One event is a pure downhill race against the clock. In the other, competitors pick their own line from a helicopter and are judged on the difficulty of the line they choose, the degree of control, and their jumps — some as big as seventy feet!

The first extreme event was held in Valdez, Alaska, in 1992, and was known as "King and Queen of the Hill." Europe hosted its first extreme championships in March 1996.

FREESTYLE JUDGING

The following is an abridged version of the ISF freestyle scoring system. It is offered as a guide to prospective competitors and spectators alike.

In halfpipe or slopestyle events, riders are judged on four criteria: non-rotational maneuvers, rotational maneuvers, height, and transitions. Here is a description of each:

NON-ROTATIONAL MANEUVERS: All moves where the rider does not rotate the board more than 180 degrees. Riders are judged on variety, degree of difficulty, combinations, and style. For a competitor to get a perfect score, at least half their maneuvers in the run must be non-rotational. Execution of the maneuvers is reflected in the score. (Examples of non-rotational airs: air to fakie, 180 alley-oop, and lip tricks.)

ROTATIONAL MANEUVERS: All moves where the rider rotates the board 360 degrees or more. Riders are judged on variety, degree of difficulty, combinations, and style. For a competitor to achieve a perfect score, the rotational maneuvers must have a high degree of difficulty and be performed flawlessly. (Examples of rotational airs: 360, 720,

900 frontside and backside airs, McTwist and the Haakon Flip.)

HEIGHT: The height score is an average height of all the maneuvers of the run. Consistency is the key. The biggest air of the day may not get the highest score in this category. Height is measured from the rider's center of gravity and not the height of the board. Execution is not reflected in this score.

TRANSITION: This category includes everything between the start to the finish line that isn't a maneuver. Competitors are scored from the end of one maneuver to the beginning of their next, for smoothness, fluidity, control, and style. This score also reflects creative use of the terrain, or pipe, which includes the quantity of maneuvers performed.

In **BIG AIR** contests, riders are judged on height, degree of difficulty, and control, which includes the landing.

GLOSSARY

AIRS: Jumps on a snowboard. "Getting air under your board" is an expression that evolved from skateboarding and surfing.

ALLEY-OOP: A term borrowed from skateboarding. It refers to a backside 360, off the toe edge.

BACKSIDE: Usually refers to a turn or spin where the spin is in the direction of the back of the board.

BACKSIDE GRAB: When you grab your heelside edge, usually between your bindings, with your front hand.

BONED OUT: Refers to a freestyle move where one leg is fully straightened.

CARVING: A turn where the board is on its edge and tracing a narrow line in the snow. A carved turn is a high-control, high-performance turn.

CAT-BOARDING: A rapidly growing industry where specially tracked vehicles (cats) take snowboarders into the backcountry for fresh powder descents.

DUCK STANCE: A centred riding stance where the front and back angles are equal and opposite (for example, +10 and -10). This stance is not for everyone, so experiment.

FAKIE: Riding backwards. It's name has its roots in skateboarding.

FALLLINE: The path a ball would follow if you let it roll down a slope.

FAT: big, large, huge – refers to airs, not pants.

FIS: Federation Internationale du Ski. This is the governing body of all alpine ski events and of a professional snowboarding tour that parallels the ISF's. FIS is the snowboarding governing body for the 1998 Nagano Winter Olympics.

FRONTSIDE: Usually refers to a turn or spin where the spin is in the direction of the front of the board.

GOOFY: A goofy-foot rider is one that is most

comfortable riding with his or her right foot forward.

GRAB: When you grab your board during an air. There are four basic airs: mute, indy, backside, and method.

HAAKON FLIP: A halfpipe trick named after freestyle sensation Terje Haakonsen of Norway. A Haakon Flip is like a McTwist, except you take off switch, spin 720, and land normal.

HITS: Snow jumps. They come in many shapes and sizes, from snowy stumps to cliffs.

HEELSIDE: Used to describe a turn on the heel edge of your board.

HELI-BOARDING: A rapidly growing industry where specially equipped helicopters take snowboarders into the backcountry for fresh powder descents.

INDY GRAB: When you grab your toe-side edge with your back hand.

INSERTS: Stainless steel mounting hardware to hold your bindings on the board.

ISF: International Snowboard Federation. The governing body that oversees the development of snowboarding worldwide. It is for snowboarders and is run by snowboarders.

LIFTIE: A lift operator.

LIP: The crest of a jump. This is where you should be at your maximum extension to get maximum air time.

MCTWIST: This trick is performed in a halfpipe. It is an inverted trick (a back flip) where you spin 540 degrees backside. You take off regular and land normal.

METHOD: An air where you grab your board with your front hand, in front of your forward binding, and kick out the tail of the board while arching your body. This is the mule kick of snowboarding and is a staple move.

MISTY FLIP: This is like a McTwist (inverted 540), except it's performed off a straight jump. You take off normal and land fakie.

MUTE GRAB: When you grab your toe-side edge, between your bindings, with your front hand.

NOSEROLL: A 180-degree pivot on the nose of your board. Commonly used to get into riding fakie.

OFF-PISTE: Refers to the backcountry, off the commonly ridden path, but not out of bounds.

P-TEX: The base material of your board. It's a plastic and comes in either extruded or sintered grades, but sintered is better. Bases also have a number that indicates quality. The higher the number, the higher the quality. A good board should have at least a sintered 1,000 base.

RODEO FLIP: Like the Misty Flip, this inverted 540 to fakie is performed off a straight jump, but the spin is frontside.

SLIDING TURN: A turn where the tail of the board slides through the last phase of the turn. These are the turns of choice in moguls and on steeps, where controlling your speed is necessary.

SNAKE: To cut in front, or ride out of turn. ("That Homer snaked the jump and bailed!")

SWING WEIGHT: Refers to the feel a board has when spinning in the air, and is of concern to freestyle riders. The lower the swing weight, the easier it is to spin the board.

SWITCH: When you perform a trick from fakie, you are doing the trick switch.

TAILROLL: A 180-degree pivot on the tail of your board. Commonly used to go from fakie riding to regular.

TOESIDE: Used to describe a turn on the toe edge of your board.

TWEAKING: Contorting one's body in very stylish ways. Not recommended for the elderly.

INDEX